Green and Sustainable Logistics and Supply Chain Management

Hand Guide for Professionals and Students

Arthur Wilson

Copyright © Arthur Wilson

Cover picture designed by Freepik.com

All rights reserved. No part of this publication may be reproduced, distributed, or transmitted in any form or by any means, including photocopying, recording, or other electronic or mechanical methods, without the prior written permission of the publisher, except in the case of brief quotations embodied in critical reviews and certain other noncommercial uses permitted by copyright law.

This book is based on extensive research, personal experience and reliable sources.

ISBN: 9798853340664

Independently published in 2023

General Information:

In the face of pressing environmental challenges and growing consumer demand for ethical products, sustainability has emerged as a defining factor in the modern business landscape. Industries worldwide are acknowledging the urgent need to embrace responsible practices, and the supply chain sector is no exception. With its extensive reach across the global economy, the supply chain plays a pivotal role in shaping the planet's future.

This book delves into the critical journey towards a sustainable and responsible supply chain. It explores the transformative power of integrating eco-friendly initiatives and ethical considerations into every facet of the supply chain, from sourcing and manufacturing to distribution and end-of-life disposal.

Over the past few decades, our planet has faced the mounting consequences of unsustainable practices, ranging from resource depletion and pollution to climate change. As these challenges escalate, businesses have come to realize that they have a profound responsibility to act as stewards of the environment and society. The supply chain, often referred to as the backbone of business operations, plays an instrumental role in this mission.

Through the pages of this book, we will navigate the complexities and opportunities inherent in building a sustainable supply chain. We will explore how responsible sourcing and manufacturing can minimize environmental impact and promote social welfare. We will delve into the role of technology and innovation in driving eco-friendly logistics and optimizing resource utilization. Moreover, we will examine the significance of collaborative efforts between stakeholders to create a collective impact in achieving sustainable goals.

The journey towards sustainability in the supply chain is not just an aspiration; it is an imperative for securing a more resilient and thriving future. This book aims to be a guiding light for supply chain professionals, business leaders, students, and anyone invested in nurturing ethical pathways in the supply chain sector. Together, we will uncover the potential for positive change, driven by a shared commitment to sustainability and a collective vision for a better world.

As we embark on this transformative expedition, let us take the first step towards a more sustainable and equitable supply chain, one that leaves a lasting legacy for generations to come. With each chapter, we will gain insights, explore best practices, and envision a future where sustainability in the supply chain is not just an ideal, but a way of life. Join me as we embark on this journey, and together, we will nurture a world that balances prosperity, people, and the planet.

Introduction of the Author (Arthur Wilson):

Arthur Wilson is a distinguished logistics professional with over three decades of experience in the Supply Chain, Logistics and international trade sectors. His career journey began as a freight forwarder, where he developed a passion for the complexities and opportunities in the logistics industry. Over the years, he honed his expertise, working with leading airfreight carriers, global logistics companies, and international organizations.

Arthur's deep knowledge of sustainable logistics and dedication to advancing the industry led him to serve on various industry committees and contribute to policy discussions. His contributions have not only improved logistics operations but have also enhanced the industry's sustainability efforts and regulatory compliance.

Recognized for his thought leadership, Arthur is a sought-after speaker at industry conferences, sharing his insights on trends, emerging technologies, and best practices. His commitment to empowering future generations of logisticians led him to mentor and guide aspiring professionals, fostering a legacy of excellence in the field.

In " Green and Sustainable Logistics and Supply Chain Management, Hand Guide for Professionals and Students," Arthur Wilson brings his wealth of knowledge and expertise to readers, offering an authoritative and engaging exploration of sustainability in the Supply Chain sector. With a profound understanding of the challenges and opportunities, Arthur's writing bridges the gap between theoretical concepts and practical applications, making this book an invaluable resource for logistics professionals and students.

Contents

General Information: 3
Introduction of the Author (Arthur Wilson): 6
Chapter 1: Introduction 12
   1.1 The Importance of Green Logistics 12
   1.2 The Environmental Impact of Traditional Logistics 13
   1.3 The Need for Sustainable Solutions 15
   1.4. Conclusion 17
Chapter 2: Understanding Green Logistics 18
   2.1 Defining Green Logistics 18
   2.2 The Core Principles of Green Logistics 19
   2.3 Environmental Benefits and Business Advantages 21
   2.4. Conclusion 24
Chapter 3: Green Transportation 26
   3.1 Alternative Fuel Vehicles: Electric, Hybrid, and Hydrogen 26
   3.2 Optimizing Route Planning for Fuel Efficiency 28
   3.3 Sustainable Transportation Modes: Rail, Water, and Air 29
   3.4. Conclusion 31
Chapter 4: Efficient Warehousing and Packaging 32
   4.1 Sustainable Warehouse Design and Operations ... 32
   4.2 Eco-Friendly Packaging Materials and Design 34
   4.3 Minimizing Waste and Recycling Initiatives 36

4.4. Conclusion 38

Chapter 5: Renewable Energy Integration...................... 40

    5.1 Adopting Renewable Energy Sources in Logistics Operations... 40

    5.2 Solar and Wind Energy Applications in Warehouses and Transportation... 42

    5.3 Energy Management and Storage Solutions.......... 43

    5.4. Conclusion 45

Chapter 6: Green Supply Chain Management 46

    6.1 Integrating Sustainability into Supply Chain Strategies.. 46

    6.2 Supplier Selection and Green Procurement Practices 48

    6.3 Collaboration and Partnerships for Sustainable Supply Chains... 49

    6.4. Conclusion 51

Chapter 7: Technology and Innovation in Green Logistics 52

    7.1 Internet of Things (IoT) and Smart Logistics 52

    7.2 Big Data Analytics for Sustainable Decision Making 54

    7.3 Blockchain for Transparency and Traceability........ 55

    7.4. Conclusion 57

Chapter 8: Environmental Regulations and Compliance. 58

    8.1 Understanding Environmental Laws Impacting Logistics 58

8.2 Reporting and Measuring Carbon Footprint......... 60

8.3 Best Practices for Meeting Regulatory Standards . 61

8.4 Conclusion 64

Chapter 9: Green Logistics Case Studies 66

9.1 Successful Implementation of Green Logistics Strategies... 66

Case Study 1: Company X - Electrification of Delivery Fleet... 66

Case Study 2: Company Y - Sustainable Packaging Solutions 67

9.2 Lessons from Leading Sustainable Companies 69

Case Study 3: Company Z - Collaborative Green Initiatives.. 69

9.3 Real-World Examples of Environmental and Financial Gains... 70

Case Study 4: Company A - Waste Recycling Program 70

Case Study 5: Company B - Renewable Energy Integration... 71

9.4. Conclusion 73

Chapter 10: The Cost of Pollution 74

Case Study 1: Exxon Valdez Oil Spill........................ 74

Case Study 2: Maersk Line and the "Low Sulphur Fuel Surcharge" 78

Case Study 3: Nestlé and the Palm Oil Supply Chain 83

Chapter 11: Challenges and Future Trends 88

   11.1 Overcoming Obstacles in Adopting Green Logistics 88

   11.2 The Role of Government and Policy Changes 90

   11.3 Emerging Technologies and Trends in Sustainability 91

   11.4. Conclusion 93

Chapter 12: Human-Centered Sustainability in the Supply Chain 96

   12.1 The Human Face of the Supply Chain.................. 96

   12.2 Empowering Communities and Local Economies 97

   12.3 Ethical Sourcing and Responsible Supplier Relationships 98

   12.4 Diversity and Inclusion in the Supply Chain Workforce 98

   12.5 Health and Well-being of Supply Chain Workers 99

   12.6 Upskilling and Training for Sustainable Employment 99

   12.7 Stakeholder Collaboration for Human-Centered Sustainability 100

   12.8 Conclusion 100

Chapter 13: Conclusion 102

   13.1 Recap of Key Green Logistics Principles............ 102

   13.2 The Roadmap to a Greener Logistics Industry .. 103

   13.3 Inspiring a Sustainable Future in Logistics 105

Chapter 1: Introduction

In an ever-changing world that increasingly values sustainability and environmental consciousness, the logistics industry faces a pressing need to embrace greener practices. This chapter delves into the significance of green logistics, highlighting the environmental impact of traditional logistics and underscoring the urgency for sustainable solutions.

1.1 The Importance of Green Logistics

Green logistics, also known as sustainable logistics or eco-logistics, refers to the integration of environmentally friendly principles and practices into the entire supply chain management process. It entails reducing carbon emissions, minimizing waste, conserving resources, and employing innovative technologies to create a more sustainable and eco-conscious logistics ecosystem.

The importance of green logistics lies in its potential to address the critical environmental challenges that our planet faces today. As logistics operations play a substantial role in greenhouse gas emissions, resource consumption, and waste generation, transitioning to sustainable logistics practices can significantly contribute to mitigating climate change and fostering environmental preservation.

Moreover, green logistics goes beyond environmental benefits; it also yields various economic advantages for companies. By optimizing energy consumption, streamlining operations, and adopting sustainable materials, businesses can achieve cost savings, enhanced efficiency, and a competitive edge in the market.

1.2 The Environmental Impact of Traditional Logistics

Traditional logistics, while essential for global trade and economic development, has a substantial impact on the environment. The use of fossil fuels in transportation, such as diesel-powered trucks and ships, leads to significant carbon dioxide (CO_2) emissions, contributing to air pollution and climate change.

Additionally, the excessive consumption of resources in the logistics process, including water and packaging materials, depletes natural reserves and exacerbates ecological degradation. The improper disposal of waste generated from packaging and transportation further adds to the environmental burden, polluting land and water bodies.

The reliance on non-renewable energy sources and inefficient supply chain management practices also results in unnecessary greenhouse gas emissions and contributes to the depletion of finite resources.

1.3 The Need for Sustainable Solutions

The need for sustainable logistics solutions has never been more urgent. As the world faces the consequences of environmental degradation, including extreme weather events, rising sea levels, and loss of biodiversity, there is a collective responsibility to adopt more eco-friendly practices in every aspect of life, including logistics.

Businesses, governments, and consumers alike are recognizing the value of sustainability in preserving the planet for future generations. The logistics industry, as a significant player in the global economy, has a unique opportunity and responsibility to lead the way in mitigating environmental impact.

By embracing green logistics practices, companies can not only reduce their carbon footprint but also demonstrate their commitment to corporate social responsibility and environmental stewardship.

Sustainable logistics initiatives can improve a company's reputation, attract environmentally conscious customers, and foster a positive organizational culture.

1.4. Conclusion

In conclusion, green logistics is not just a buzzword or a passing trend; it is an imperative shift towards a more sustainable and responsible approach to managing the flow of goods and materials. Throughout this book, we will explore the principles, strategies, and real-world examples of green logistics that demonstrate its potential to create a positive impact on both the environment and businesses.

In the following chapters, we will delve into specific aspects of green logistics, ranging from green transportation and efficient warehousing to renewable energy integration and the use of technology in sustainable logistics practices. Together, let us explore the path towards a greener future for the logistics industry.

Chapter 2: Understanding Green Logistics

Logistics has evolved beyond mere transportation and warehousing; it now incorporates a fundamental commitment to sustainability. In this chapter, we explore the concept of green logistics, its core principles, and the environmental and business advantages it offers.

2.1 Defining Green Logistics

Green logistics, often referred to as sustainable logistics or eco-logistics, is an approach to supply chain management that prioritizes environmental responsibility and social consciousness. It encompasses a wide range of practices aimed at reducing the negative impact of logistics operations on the environment while optimizing efficiency and maintaining economic viability.

At its core, green logistics seeks to minimize carbon emissions, energy consumption, waste generation, and resource depletion throughout the supply chain. This includes embracing alternative transportation methods, adopting renewable energy sources, implementing eco-friendly warehousing and packaging, and making informed decisions based on environmental considerations.

Green logistics extends beyond individual companies; it involves collaboration among all stakeholders in the supply chain, including manufacturers, suppliers, carriers, and end consumers. By fostering cooperation and collective efforts, the logistics industry can collectively contribute to a more sustainable and greener future.

2.2 The Core Principles of Green Logistics

(i) Reducing Emissions: One of the central principles of green logistics is the reduction of greenhouse gas emissions. This is achieved by employing energy-efficient vehicles, optimizing transportation routes, and encouraging the use of alternative fuel technologies such as electric, hybrid, or hydrogen-powered vehicles.

(ii) Efficient Resource Management: Green logistics focuses on responsible resource management to minimize waste and reduce resource consumption. This includes effective inventory management to avoid overstocking, the use of eco-friendly packaging materials, and recycling and reusing materials whenever possible.

(iii) Sustainable Warehousing: Green logistics promotes sustainable warehousing practices that optimize space utilization, utilize renewable energy sources, and implement efficient heating, cooling, and lighting systems. Sustainable warehouses are designed to minimize their environmental impact and ensure the responsible handling of goods.

(iv) Collaborative Supply Chain: Collaboration and communication among supply chain partners are essential in green logistics. By sharing information, coordinating efforts, and collectively aiming for sustainability goals, supply chain stakeholders can work together to create a more eco-friendly and efficient supply chain.

(v) Transparency and Traceability: Green logistics encourages transparency throughout the supply chain, enabling stakeholders and consumers to trace the environmental impact of products from sourcing to delivery. Transparency fosters accountability and motivates companies to make environmentally conscious decisions.

2.3 Environmental Benefits and Business Advantages

The adoption of green logistics practices offers a myriad of benefits, both for the environment and for businesses operating in the logistics industry.

Environmental Benefits:

Reduced Carbon Footprint: Green logistics significantly lowers greenhouse gas emissions, contributing to climate change mitigation and improved air quality.

Resource Conservation: Sustainable practices lead to reduced consumption of natural resources, preserving them for future generations.

Waste Reduction: Green logistics minimizes waste generation and promotes recycling and responsible disposal, reducing environmental pollution.

Biodiversity Preservation: By reducing the ecological impact of logistics operations, green logistics helps protect biodiversity and fragile ecosystems.

Business Advantages:

Cost Savings: Energy-efficient practices and waste reduction measures lead to cost savings in fuel, energy, and materials.

Competitive Edge: Companies that embrace green logistics gain a competitive advantage, appealing to environmentally conscious consumers and stakeholders.

Brand Reputation: Green logistics enhances a company's reputation and strengthens its brand image as an environmentally responsible entity.

Regulatory Compliance: Sustainable practices align with increasingly stringent environmental regulations, ensuring compliance and avoiding penalties.

2.4. Conclusion

In the pursuit of green logistics, businesses can contribute positively to the environment while also reaping the rewards of improved efficiency, cost savings, and enhanced market positioning. The next chapters will delve deeper into specific areas of green logistics, exploring strategies, technologies, and real-world examples that exemplify its implementation in the logistics industry.

Chapter 3: Green Transportation

Transportation is a significant contributor to carbon emissions and environmental degradation in the logistics industry. In this chapter, we explore various green transportation solutions aimed at reducing the environmental impact of moving goods and materials.

3.1 Alternative Fuel Vehicles: Electric, Hybrid, and Hydrogen

One of the key strategies in green transportation is the adoption of alternative fuel vehicles that produce fewer emissions compared to traditional fossil fuel-powered vehicles.

(i) Electric Vehicles (EVs): Electric vehicles are powered by electric motors and use rechargeable batteries as their energy source. They produce zero tailpipe emissions, making them a clean and environmentally friendly option. With advancements in battery technology and the growing availability of charging infrastructure, electric trucks, vans, and even cargo ships are becoming viable options in the logistics industry.

(ii) Hybrid Vehicles: Hybrid vehicles combine both internal combustion engines (typically gasoline or diesel) and electric motors. They can operate on electric power for short distances, reducing fuel consumption and emissions during stop-and-go traffic or low-speed driving. Hybrid trucks and delivery vans are being integrated into logistics fleets to improve fuel efficiency and lower emissions.

(iii) Hydrogen Fuel Cell Vehicles: Hydrogen fuel cell vehicles use hydrogen gas to produce electricity, which powers the vehicle's electric motor. The only byproduct of this process is water vapor, making hydrogen fuel cell vehicles emissions-free. Although still in the early stages of adoption, hydrogen-powered trucks and buses show promise as an environmentally friendly transportation option.

3.2 Optimizing Route Planning for Fuel Efficiency

Efficient route planning plays a crucial role in reducing fuel consumption and emissions during transportation.

(i) GPS and Routing Software: Advanced GPS systems and routing software enable logistics companies to optimize delivery routes based on real-time traffic information, road conditions, and weather. By choosing the most fuel-efficient routes, companies can save on fuel costs and minimize emissions.

(ii) Consolidation and Backhauling: By consolidating shipments and planning backhauling trips (carrying return loads on the back leg of a journey), logistics companies can maximize the capacity of their vehicles and reduce the number of empty or partially filled trips, leading to lower emissions per unit of cargo transported.

(iii) Intermodal Transportation: Utilizing intermodal transportation, which combines multiple transportation modes like rail, truck, and ship, can lead to greater fuel efficiency and reduced emissions for long-distance hauls. Rail and water transportation are generally more energy-efficient than long-haul trucking, especially for bulk shipments.

3.3 Sustainable Transportation Modes: Rail, Water, and Air

Beyond alternative fuel vehicles and efficient route planning, embracing sustainable transportation modes can significantly reduce the carbon footprint of logistics operations.

(i) Rail Transportation: Rail transport is highly energy-efficient and emits fewer greenhouse gases per ton-mile compared to road transportation. For long-distance transportation of bulk goods, such as minerals, grains, and raw materials, trains offer a greener alternative to trucks.

(ii) Water Transportation: Shipping goods via waterways, such as oceans, seas, and rivers, is one of the most environmentally friendly modes of transportation. Large cargo vessels can carry a massive amount of freight, reducing emissions per unit of cargo significantly. Inland waterways and coastal shipping also provide green alternatives for domestic transport.

(iii) Air Cargo Efficiency: While air transportation is often associated with higher emissions, improvements in air cargo efficiency and optimization can help mitigate its impact. Employing newer, more fuel-efficient aircraft and optimizing cargo loading and routing can reduce the environmental impact of air freight.

3.4. Conclusion

By implementing these green transportation strategies, logistics companies can make significant strides towards sustainability while still meeting their delivery obligations. In the next chapters, we will delve further into other aspects of green logistics, such as eco-friendly warehousing, renewable energy integration, and collaboration for a more sustainable supply chain.

Chapter 4: Efficient Warehousing and Packaging

Efficient warehousing and eco-friendly packaging are integral components of green logistics. This chapter explores sustainable warehouse design and operations, eco-friendly packaging materials and design, as well as waste minimization and recycling initiatives that contribute to a greener and more environmentally responsible logistics industry.

4.1 Sustainable Warehouse Design and Operations

Sustainable warehouse design and operations focus on reducing energy consumption, optimizing space utilization, and minimizing the environmental impact of warehousing activities.

(i) Energy-Efficient Lighting: Implementing energy-efficient lighting systems, such as LED or motion-activated lighting, can significantly reduce electricity usage and lower greenhouse gas emissions.

(ii) Renewable Energy Integration: Utilizing renewable energy sources, such as solar panels and wind turbines, can power warehouse operations and reduce reliance on fossil fuels.

(iii) Energy Management Systems: Deploying energy management systems allows warehouses to monitor and control energy usage, identifying areas for improvement and optimizing energy consumption.

(iv) Optimized Racking and Storage: Using smart racking systems and storage solutions ensures efficient space utilization, reducing the need for expansive warehouse footprints and the associated environmental impact.

(v) Green Construction Materials: Constructing or retrofitting warehouses using environmentally friendly materials, such as recycled steel and sustainable insulation, promotes green building practices.

(vi) Natural Ventilation and Cooling: Employing natural ventilation and cooling techniques, like strategically placed vents and passive cooling methods, can reduce reliance on air conditioning systems and lower energy consumption.

4.2 Eco-Friendly Packaging Materials and Design

Eco-friendly packaging is crucial in minimizing the environmental impact of shipping and reducing waste in the supply chain.

(i) Biodegradable and Compostable Materials: Adopting biodegradable and compostable packaging materials, such as plant-based plastics and biodegradable bubble wraps, ensures that packaging waste breaks down naturally over time.

(ii) Recycled Packaging: Using recycled materials for packaging, including cardboard, paper, and plastic, reduces the demand for virgin materials and conserves natural resources.

(iii) Right-Sizing Packaging: Implementing the right-sizing of packages to match the dimensions of the product being shipped reduces the use of excess materials and minimizes empty space in shipping boxes.

(iv) Minimalist Design: Simplifying packaging design and avoiding unnecessary layers or non-recyclable elements can reduce waste and environmental impact.

(v) Reusable Packaging: Implementing reusable packaging solutions, such as durable totes and containers, promotes a circular economy approach and reduces the need for single-use packaging.

4.3 Minimizing Waste and Recycling Initiatives

Efforts to minimize waste and encourage recycling in warehouses and throughout the supply chain are essential components of green logistics.

(i) Waste Audits: Conducting regular waste audits allows warehouses to identify areas where waste can be reduced and develop targeted waste minimization strategies.

(ii) Waste Segregation: Implementing proper waste segregation practices ensures that recyclable materials are separated from general waste, facilitating more efficient recycling processes.

(iii) Recycling Partnerships: Collaborating with recycling partners and waste management companies enables warehouses to ensure that recyclable materials are properly processed.

(iv) Product Returns Management: Implementing efficient product returns management processes can help reduce waste and prevent unnecessary disposal of returned items.

(v) Circular Economy Initiatives: Encouraging circular economy practices, such as product refurbishment and recycling, ensures that resources are kept in use for as long as possible, minimizing waste and resource depletion.

4.4. Conclusion

By prioritizing efficient warehousing and eco-friendly packaging, logistics companies can significantly reduce their environmental impact and move closer to achieving sustainable supply chain operations. In the subsequent chapters, we will explore other aspects of green logistics, including renewable energy integration, sustainable supply chain management, and the role of technology in fostering eco-friendly practices.

Chapter 5: Renewable Energy Integration

As the world shifts towards a more sustainable future, the logistics industry can play a vital role by adopting renewable energy sources. This chapter explores the integration of renewable energy in logistics operations, with a focus on solar and wind energy applications in warehouses and transportation, as well as energy management and storage solutions.

5.1 Adopting Renewable Energy Sources in Logistics Operations

The adoption of renewable energy sources is a critical step towards reducing the carbon footprint of logistics operations. By transitioning from fossil fuels to renewable energy, logistics companies can significantly decrease greenhouse gas emissions and contribute to a cleaner and greener environment.

(i) Solar Power: Installing solar panels on the rooftops of warehouses and distribution centers allows logistics facilities to harness sunlight and convert it into electricity. Solar power systems not only provide a renewable energy source but can also lead to significant cost savings on electricity bills.

(ii) Wind Power: For logistics companies situated in windy regions, wind turbines can be a viable renewable energy solution. Wind power can be harnessed to generate electricity for on-site use, helping to offset the energy demand of warehouses and distribution centers.

(iii) Biogas and Biomass: Some logistics facilities can explore the use of biogas and biomass as renewable energy sources. Biogas is produced from the decomposition of organic waste, while biomass can be derived from sustainable forestry and agricultural practices.

5.2 Solar and Wind Energy Applications in Warehouses and Transportation

Renewable energy integration extends beyond just powering warehouses; it can also be applied to various aspects of transportation.

(i) Solar-Powered Vehicles: In addition to using solar energy for stationary facilities, logistics companies can also consider adopting solar-powered vehicles. Solar panels can be integrated into the body of trucks and vans, assisting in charging their batteries and reducing fuel consumption during transit.

(ii) Solar-Powered Charging Stations: Logistics companies can establish solar-powered charging stations for electric vehicles in their fleet. These charging stations can be strategically located along transportation routes to facilitate long-haul electric transportation.

(iii) Wind-Powered Ships: In the maritime sector, some innovative designs explore the use of wind power to supplement traditional ship propulsion. Auxiliary wind sails and other wind-assisted technologies can reduce fuel consumption and emissions during sea voyages.

5.3 Energy Management and Storage Solutions

Efficient energy management and energy storage play a crucial role in making the most of renewable energy resources.

(i) Smart Grids and Energy Management Systems: Implementing smart grids and energy management systems allow logistics facilities to optimize energy usage, monitor consumption patterns, and make data-driven decisions to reduce waste.

(ii) Battery Energy Storage: Installing battery energy storage systems enables logistics companies to store excess energy generated from renewable sources and use it during peak demand or when the primary renewable source is unavailable.

(iii) Hydrogen Fuel Cells: Hydrogen fuel cells can serve as energy storage solutions, converting excess renewable energy into hydrogen gas. The stored hydrogen can then be used to power fuel cell vehicles or other equipment during periods of low renewable energy generation.

5.4. Conclusion

By embracing renewable energy integration and making the most of available energy sources, logistics companies can significantly reduce their carbon footprint and demonstrate their commitment to sustainability. The subsequent chapters will explore other green logistics initiatives, including green supply chain management, technology applications, and environmental regulations and compliance.

Chapter 6: Green Supply Chain Management

Green supply chain management is a holistic approach that emphasizes sustainability and environmental responsibility throughout the entire supply chain. In this chapter, we delve into the importance of integrating sustainability into supply chain strategies, adopting green procurement practices, and fostering collaboration and partnerships to achieve sustainable supply chains.

6.1 Integrating Sustainability into Supply Chain Strategies

Integrating sustainability into supply chain strategies involves incorporating environmental considerations into every decision-making process along the supply chain.

(i) Life Cycle Assessments: Conducting life cycle assessments helps identify the environmental impact of products and processes at each stage, from raw material extraction to end-of-life disposal. This enables companies to make informed choices to reduce their ecological footprint.

(ii) Setting Sustainability Goals: Establishing clear and measurable sustainability goals, such as reducing carbon emissions or waste, going net zero by a specific date, serves as a roadmap for the entire supply chain to work towards a greener future.

(iii) Supplier Engagement: Collaborating with suppliers and fostering a sustainability mindset among them can lead to the adoption of eco-friendly practices and the sourcing of environmentally responsible materials.

(iv) Reverse Logistics: Implementing efficient reverse logistics processes for product returns and end-of-life management can minimize waste and encourage recycling and refurbishment.

6.2 Supplier Selection and Green Procurement Practices

Supplier selection and green procurement practices are instrumental in ensuring that sustainability principles are upheld throughout the supply chain.

(i) Sustainability Criteria in Supplier Selection: Integrating sustainability criteria into supplier selection processes enables companies to partner with suppliers who share similar environmental values and practices.

(ii) Eco-Friendly Materials Sourcing: Opting for eco-friendly materials, such as recycled or renewable materials, helps reduce the environmental impact of products and packaging.

(iii) Certifications and Standards: Seeking suppliers with recognized sustainability certifications or compliance with environmental standards ensures that environmental responsibility is upheld in the supply chain.

(iv) Collaborative Green Innovation: Encouraging suppliers to develop and implement green innovations fosters a culture of continuous improvement towards sustainability.

6.3 Collaboration and Partnerships for Sustainable Supply Chains

Sustainable supply chains require collaboration and partnerships among all stakeholders to create a collective impact.

(i) Transparency and Data Sharing: Transparently sharing sustainability data with supply chain partners enhances accountability and enables data-driven decisions to improve environmental performance.

(ii) Collaborative Initiatives: Collaborating with supply chain partners to tackle common sustainability challenges, such as reducing emissions or waste, leads to more effective and holistic solutions.

(iii) Joint Sustainability Projects: Engaging in joint sustainability projects, such as carbon offset programs or community-based environmental initiatives, demonstrates a commitment to sustainability beyond individual organizations.

(iv) Supplier Development Programs: Establishing supplier development programs that provide support and resources for suppliers to implement green practices helps create a more sustainable supply chain ecosystem.

(v) Sustainable Procurement Networks: Participating in sustainable procurement networks and industry-wide initiatives fosters knowledge sharing and the exchange of best practices for green supply chain management.

6.4. Conclusion

By prioritizing green supply chain management, companies can not only reduce their environmental impact but also create a positive reputation as responsible and ethical business entities. Collaborative efforts and partnerships within the supply chain can lead to shared success and a more sustainable future for the logistics industry.

In the upcoming chapters, we will explore the role of technology and innovation in green logistics, environmental regulations and compliance, and real-world case studies of successful green logistics implementation.

Chapter 7: Technology and Innovation in Green Logistics

Technology and innovation play a pivotal role in driving green logistics practices. In this chapter, we explore the use of the Internet of Things (IoT) and smart logistics, big data analytics for sustainable decision-making, and the application of blockchain technology for transparency and traceability in the logistics industry.

7.1 Internet of Things (IoT) and Smart Logistics

The Internet of Things (IoT) refers to the interconnected network of devices that can collect and exchange data. In logistics, IoT enables smart logistics solutions, revolutionizing the way goods are tracked, monitored, and managed throughout the supply chain.

(i) Real-Time Monitoring: IoT devices, such as sensors and GPS trackers, provide real-time visibility into the location, condition, and status of goods in transit. This enables logistics companies to optimize routes, reduce delays, and proactively address potential issues.

(ii) Condition Monitoring: IoT sensors can monitor temperature, humidity, and other environmental factors during transportation, especially in the case of sensitive or perishable goods. This helps maintain product quality and prevent spoilage or damage.

(iii) Asset Utilization: IoT-enabled asset tracking allows logistics companies to monitor and optimize the use of equipment, vehicles, and containers, reducing idle times and improving operational efficiency.

(iv) Predictive Maintenance: IoT data can be leveraged to predict maintenance needs for vehicles and equipment, enabling timely repairs and minimizing downtime, thus reducing fuel consumption and emissions.

7.2 Big Data Analytics for Sustainable Decision Making

Big data analytics involves analyzing vast amounts of data to derive valuable insights and support decision-making. In green logistics, big data analytics plays a crucial role in optimizing operations and promoting sustainability.

(i) Energy Efficiency Optimization: Big data analytics can identify patterns in energy consumption, enabling logistics companies to optimize energy usage in warehouses, transportation, and other operational processes.

(ii) Optimized Route Planning: By analyzing historical transportation data and real-time traffic information, big data analytics can suggest the most fuel-efficient routes, minimizing emissions and reducing the overall environmental impact.

(iii) Demand Forecasting: Accurate demand forecasting through big data analytics helps prevent overstocking or understocking, reducing waste and unnecessary transportation.

(iv) Carbon Footprint Tracking: Big data analytics can track and measure the carbon footprint of logistics operations, helping companies set and monitor progress towards sustainability goals.

7.3 Blockchain for Transparency and Traceability

Blockchain technology offers a decentralized and immutable ledger that enhances transparency and traceability in the supply chain.

(i) Supply Chain Transparency: Blockchain enables end-to-end visibility of the supply chain, allowing stakeholders to track products' journey from origin to destination. This transparency helps identify inefficiencies and areas for improvement.

(ii) Provenance Verification: With blockchain, companies can verify the authenticity and origin of products, ensuring adherence to sustainability and ethical sourcing standards.

(iii) Smart Contracts for Green Initiatives: Blockchain-based smart contracts can automate and enforce sustainability agreements between supply chain partners, incentivizing eco-friendly practices.

(iv) Carbon Emission Tracking: Blockchain can securely record and track carbon emissions throughout the supply chain, facilitating carbon offset programs and fostering a carbon-neutral approach.

7.4. Conclusion

By leveraging technology and innovation in green logistics, the industry can achieve higher levels of efficiency, transparency, and sustainability. The integration of IoT, big data analytics, and blockchain offers powerful tools to reduce environmental impact, make data-driven decisions, and uphold sustainability principles throughout the logistics ecosystem.

In the next chapters, we will explore environmental regulations and compliance in green logistics, real-world case studies of successful green logistics implementation, and the challenges and future trends in the pursuit of a more sustainable logistics industry.

Chapter 8: Environmental Regulations and Compliance

In an era of heightened environmental awareness, governments and international bodies have enacted various regulations to promote sustainability and reduce the environmental impact of industries, including logistics. This chapter delves into understanding environmental laws impacting logistics, reporting and measuring carbon footprint, and best practices for meeting regulatory standards.

8.1 Understanding Environmental Laws Impacting Logistics

Governments worldwide have introduced environmental laws and regulations to address climate change, resource depletion, and pollution. These regulations impact the logistics industry in several key areas:

(i) Emissions Standards: Environmental regulations set limits on emissions from vehicles, mandating logistics companies to reduce greenhouse gas emissions and promote cleaner transportation methods.

(ii) Fuel Efficiency Standards: Some regions have established fuel efficiency standards, compelling logistics companies to utilize more efficient vehicles and optimize route planning to minimize fuel consumption.

(iii) Waste Management: Environmental laws may require proper waste management practices, including recycling and disposal, to minimize the environmental impact of logistics operations.

(iv) Packaging Regulations: Regulations on packaging materials and recycling obligations encourage logistics companies to adopt eco-friendly packaging solutions and minimize packaging waste.

(v) Sustainability Reporting: Certain jurisdictions mandate sustainability reporting, where logistics companies must disclose their environmental practices, goals, and performance.

8.2 Reporting and Measuring Carbon Footprint

Measuring and reporting the carbon footprint of logistics operations is crucial for assessing environmental impact and progress toward sustainability goals.

(i) Carbon Accounting: Carbon accounting involves quantifying greenhouse gas emissions produced by various activities in the supply chain, such as transportation, warehousing, and energy consumption.

(ii) Carbon Footprint Reporting: Logistics companies may be required to report their carbon footprint regularly, either to regulatory bodies or as part of voluntary sustainability initiatives.

(iii) Carbon Offset Programs: Companies can offset their carbon emissions by investing in projects that reduce or remove an equivalent amount of carbon dioxide from the atmosphere, such as reforestation or renewable energy projects.

(iv) Environmental Impact Assessment: Conducting environmental impact assessments helps identify areas of high environmental impact within logistics operations and develop targeted sustainability strategies.

8.3 Best Practices for Meeting Regulatory Standards

Complying with environmental regulations requires proactive measures and the adoption of best practices for sustainable logistics operations.

(i) Adopting Green Technologies: Embrace eco-friendly technologies such as electric vehicles, renewable energy sources, and energy-efficient warehouse systems to meet emissions and energy standards.

(ii) Investing in Training and Awareness: Educate employees and supply chain partners about environmental regulations, sustainability goals, and best practices to foster a culture of environmental responsibility.

(iii) Supply Chain Collaboration: Collaborate with supply chain partners to implement shared sustainability initiatives and meet regulatory requirements collectively.

(iv) Continuous Improvement: Regularly assess and improve logistics processes to reduce environmental impact, incorporating feedback from stakeholders and monitoring progress toward sustainability goals.

(v) Engaging with Regulators: Stay informed about evolving environmental regulations and engage with regulatory bodies to understand compliance requirements and advocate for policies that promote green logistics.

8.4 Conclusion

By aligning with environmental regulations and adopting sustainable practices, logistics companies can not only comply with the law but also position themselves as responsible and environmentally conscious entities. Proactive efforts toward meeting regulatory standards contribute to a cleaner, more sustainable logistics industry and a positive global impact on the environment.

In the following chapters, we will explore real-world case studies of successful green logistics implementation, the challenges faced in adopting sustainable practices, and the future trends shaping the logistics industry's pursuit of sustainability.

Chapter 9: Green Logistics Case Studies

Green logistics is not just a theoretical concept; many companies have successfully implemented sustainable practices in their supply chains, resulting in both environmental and financial benefits. In this chapter, we explore case studies of successful green logistics strategies, lessons from leading sustainable companies, and real-world examples of environmental and financial gains.

9.1 Successful Implementation of Green Logistics Strategies

Case Study 1: Company X - Electrification of Delivery Fleet

Company X, a leading e-commerce retailer, implemented an ambitious green logistics strategy by electrifying its delivery fleet. They replaced a significant portion of their diesel-powered delivery vans with electric vehicles (EVs) equipped with advanced route optimization technology.

Environmental Impact: The switch to EVs led to a substantial reduction in carbon emissions, with zero tailpipe emissions during deliveries. Company X also adopted renewable energy sources for charging the EVs, further lowering their carbon footprint.

Financial Benefits: Despite the initial investment in EVs and charging infrastructure, Company X experienced long-term cost savings in fuel and maintenance. The optimized route planning also reduced mileage and improved overall fleet efficiency, resulting in lower operational expenses.

Case Study 2: Company Y - Sustainable Packaging Solutions

Company Y, a global consumer goods manufacturer, implemented sustainable packaging solutions across its supply chain.

Environmental Impact: Company Y transitioned to recyclable and biodegradable packaging materials, reducing waste generation and promoting responsible disposal practices. They also optimized packaging designs to minimize material usage without compromising product protection.

Financial Benefits: Although there was a minor upfront cost associated with redesigning packaging and sourcing eco-friendly materials, Company Y achieved significant cost savings due to reduced packaging material expenses and lower waste disposal costs. The company's commitment to sustainability also resonated with environmentally conscious consumers, leading to increased brand loyalty and market share.

9.2 Lessons from Leading Sustainable Companies

Case Study 3: Company Z- Collaborative Green Initiatives

Company Z, a logistics service provider, demonstrated the power of collaboration in achieving green logistics goals.

Lessons Learned: Company Z formed partnerships with its major suppliers, carriers, and customers to create a collaborative green initiative. Together, they established shared sustainability goals, such as emissions reduction and waste minimization, and jointly invested in sustainable technologies and practices.

Environmental Impact: Through collaboration, Company Z was able to optimize transportation routes, reduce empty miles, and consolidate shipments, resulting in a significant decrease in carbon emissions and resource consumption throughout the supply chain.

Financial Benefits: The collaborative approach improved overall supply chain efficiency and reduced operational costs for all involved parties. Company Z gained a competitive advantage by promoting its green logistics initiatives, attracting environmentally conscious customers and new business opportunities.

9.3 Real-World Examples of Environmental and Financial Gains

Case Study 4: Company A- Waste Recycling Program

Company A, a logistics company operating in the retail sector, implemented a comprehensive waste recycling program across its distribution centers.

Environmental Impact: The waste recycling program facilitated the proper segregation and recycling of paper, cardboard, plastic, and other materials, reducing the amount of waste sent to landfills. Additionally, the program encouraged responsible disposal of hazardous materials, minimizing environmental pollution.

Financial Benefits: Company A achieved cost savings through reduced waste disposal fees and lower waste management expenses. The company's commitment to sustainability also improved its brand reputation, leading to increased customer loyalty and support from eco-conscious consumers.

Case Study 5: Company B- Renewable Energy Integration

Company B, a transportation and logistics provider, integrated renewable energy sources into its operations.

Environmental Impact: Company B installed solar panels on the roofs of its warehouses and adopted a fleet of electric trucks for last-mile deliveries. The renewable energy integration significantly reduced the company's carbon footprint and dependence on fossil fuels.

Financial Benefits: Although the initial investment in renewable energy technology required capital, Company B experienced long-term cost savings on electricity bills and fuel expenses. The transition to electric trucks also attracted government incentives and tax benefits for adopting green transportation solutions.

9.4. Conclusion

These case studies highlight that sustainable logistics practices can result in tangible environmental benefits and financial gains for companies. Successful implementation of green logistics strategies requires a combination of technology adoption, collaboration, and a commitment to environmental responsibility. By learning from leading sustainable companies and real-world examples, the logistics industry can continue its journey towards a greener and more sustainable future.

In the following chapter, we will explore the challenges and potential obstacles in adopting sustainable practices, and discuss how the logistics industry can overcome these hurdles to fully embrace green logistics.

Chapter 10: The Cost of Pollution

Case Study 1: Exxon Valdez Oil Spill

On March 24, 1989, the Exxon Valdez oil tanker, operated by Exxon Shipping Company, ran aground in Prince William Sound, Alaska, resulting in one of the most devastating environmental disasters in history. The tanker spilled approximately 11 million gallons (approximately 41.6 million liters) of crude oil into the pristine waters of the Sound, creating an ecological catastrophe that had far-reaching consequences for the environment, wildlife, and the reputation of Exxon.

Environmental Impact:

The Exxon Valdez oil spill had a catastrophic impact on the fragile ecosystem of Prince William Sound and its surrounding areas. The spilled oil contaminated over 1,300 miles (approximately 2,092 kilometers) of coastline, including numerous critical habitats for marine life, birds, and other wildlife. The oil spread rapidly, affecting marine mammals, fish, and seabirds, leading to mass mortalities and long-term ecological disruptions.

Regulatory and Legal Consequences:

In the aftermath of the spill, Exxon faced intense scrutiny and legal action from government agencies, environmental groups, and affected communities. The company was found to have violated multiple environmental regulations, leading to a protracted legal battle that lasted for decades.

Exxon was held liable for billions of dollars in fines and settlements, including cleanup costs, natural resource damages, and compensation for economic losses suffered by local communities dependent on fishing and tourism.

Financial Impact:

The financial consequences of the Exxon Valdez oil spill were staggering. The total cost of the spill and its aftermath, including cleanup efforts, legal settlements, and fines, amounted to over $3.8 billion. The incident also caused a significant decline in Exxon's stock value and led to a loss of investor confidence.

Reputation and Brand Image:

The Exxon Valdez oil spill severely tarnished Exxon's reputation and brand image. The company was widely criticized for its slow response to the disaster and perceived lack of accountability. Consumers, environmental activists, and the general public held Exxon responsible for the environmental devastation and demanded greater corporate responsibility.

The spill left a lasting stain on Exxon's image, making it a cautionary tale of the consequences of neglecting environmental protection and sustainability in the supply chain.

The Path to Redemption:

In the wake of the Exxon Valdez oil spill, Exxon implemented extensive changes to its operations and practices. The company invested in advanced technology and improved safety measures to prevent future accidents. It also established initiatives focused on environmental stewardship and community engagement to rebuild trust with stakeholders.

Lessons Learned:

The Exxon Valdez oil spill serves as a vivid reminder of the immense cost of pollution in the supply chain sector. It highlights the importance of prioritizing environmental responsibility and implementing stringent measures to prevent such disasters.

This real-life case study underscores the need for robust risk management, environmental compliance, and proactive sustainability efforts within the supply chain. It exemplifies the lasting impact that pollution can have on the environment, communities, and a company's reputation. As we explore sustainability in the supply chain, the lessons from the Exxon Valdez oil spill case study remind us of the urgency and significance of adopting responsible practices to protect our planet and ensure a more sustainable future.

Case Study 2: Maersk Line and the "Low Sulphur Fuel Surcharge"

Maersk Line, a prominent global logistics company and one of the largest container shipping companies in the world, faced a significant environmental and financial challenge related to the cost of pollution in the shipping industry.

Background:

In 2015, the International Maritime Organization (IMO) introduced regulations to address air pollution caused by shipping vessels. The new regulations aimed to reduce the sulphur content in marine fuels to curb emissions of sulphur oxides (SOx), a harmful air pollutant known to contribute to respiratory and environmental issues. The regulation set a global cap on the sulphur content in marine fuels at 0.5%, down from the previous limit of 3.5%, and required shipping companies to comply by January 1, 2020.

Environmental Impact:

Prior to the new regulations, many shipping vessels, including some in Maersk Line's fleet, used high-sulphur fuel, which emitted significant amounts of SOx into the atmosphere. This contributed to air pollution, especially in heavily-trafficked shipping lanes and near port cities, leading to adverse health effects and environmental degradation in coastal regions.

Regulatory and Legal Consequences:

As the deadline for compliance with the new regulations approached, Maersk Line faced the challenge of ensuring its vessels adhered to the stringent sulphur limits. Failure to comply with the IMO regulations could result in severe penalties, including fines and potential restrictions on operating in certain regions.

To address the regulatory requirements, Maersk Line had to make strategic decisions to reduce its vessels' sulphur emissions. One approach was to switch from high-sulphur fuel to low-sulphur alternatives, such as marine gas oil (MGO) or marine diesel oil (MDO), both of which were more expensive than traditional heavy fuel oil (HFO). The switch to low-sulphur fuels meant higher operational costs for the company.

Financial Impact:

Transitioning to low-sulphur fuels came with a substantial financial burden for Maersk Line. The cost of low-sulphur fuels was significantly higher than HFO, and the company needed to budget for the increased operational expenses. To offset these costs, Maersk Line implemented a "Low Sulphur Fuel

Surcharge" to customers, adding an additional fee to cover the price difference of using low-sulphur fuels during transportation.

Reputation and Brand Image:

While Maersk Line took proactive measures to comply with the IMO regulations, the implementation of the Low Sulphur Fuel Surcharge received mixed reactions from customers and industry stakeholders. Some customers expressed concerns about the potential impact on shipping costs and the overall supply chain. The surcharge was a topic of public debate, and some critics questioned the transparency and justification of the added fee.

The Path to Redemption:

To address the reputational challenges and build trust with customers, Maersk Line communicated openly about the reasons for the fuel surcharge and the importance of complying with the IMO regulations to reduce environmental pollution. The company also continued to invest in eco-friendly technologies, exploring alternative fuel options, and optimizing its fleet to enhance fuel efficiency and further reduce its carbon footprint.

Lessons Learned:

The case of Maersk Line demonstrates the real-world challenges faced by logistics companies in addressing the cost of pollution. Compliance with environmental regulations and reducing emissions comes with significant financial implications. To navigate these challenges, companies must strike a delicate balance between environmental responsibility, operational costs, and maintaining customer satisfaction. Transparent communication and proactive efforts towards sustainability are vital for building trust with stakeholders and establishing a positive brand image in an increasingly environmentally conscious world.

Case Study 3: Nestlé and the Palm Oil Supply Chain

Nestlé, one of the world's largest food and beverage companies, faced significant environmental and reputational challenges related to the pollution caused by its palm oil supply chain.

Environmental Impact:

Palm oil is a widely used commodity in the food industry, including in Nestlé's products. However, the production of palm oil has been associated with deforestation, habitat destruction, and greenhouse gas emissions, particularly in regions like Southeast Asia where large-scale plantations are prevalent.

Nestlé's palm oil supply chain, like many others in the industry, relied on suppliers whose practices contributed to environmental degradation. The conversion of forests and peatlands for palm oil plantations led to biodiversity loss and increased carbon emissions, impacting both local ecosystems and global climate change.

Reputational Consequences:

As environmental awareness grew, consumers, NGOs, and investors began pressuring companies to address their supply chain's environmental impacts. Nestlé faced mounting criticism from stakeholders, who accused the company of contributing to deforestation and unethical practices associated with palm oil production.

In 2010, Greenpeace launched a campaign targeting Nestlé, highlighting its links to deforestation and urging the company to take action. The campaign featured a viral video showing an orangutan finger being replaced with a KitKat chocolate bar, symbolizing the impact of palm oil production on the habitat of endangered species.

Financial Impact:

Case Study 3: Nestlé and the Palm Oil Supply Chain

Nestlé, one of the world's largest food and beverage companies, faced significant environmental and reputational challenges related to the pollution caused by its palm oil supply chain.

Environmental Impact:

Palm oil is a widely used commodity in the food industry, including in Nestlé's products. However, the production of palm oil has been associated with deforestation, habitat destruction, and greenhouse gas emissions, particularly in regions like Southeast Asia where large-scale plantations are prevalent.

Nestlé's palm oil supply chain, like many others in the industry, relied on suppliers whose practices contributed to environmental degradation. The conversion of forests and peatlands for palm oil plantations led to biodiversity loss and increased carbon emissions, impacting both local ecosystems and global climate change.

Reputational Consequences:

As environmental awareness grew, consumers, NGOs, and investors began pressuring companies to address their supply chain's environmental impacts. Nestlé faced mounting criticism from stakeholders, who accused the company of contributing to deforestation and unethical practices associated with palm oil production.

In 2010, Greenpeace launched a campaign targeting Nestlé, highlighting its links to deforestation and urging the company to take action. The campaign featured a viral video showing an orangutan finger being replaced with a KitKat chocolate bar, symbolizing the impact of palm oil production on the habitat of endangered species.

Financial Impact:

The reputational damage resulting from the palm oil supply chain issues had financial implications for Nestlé. The negative publicity and consumer backlash affected sales and brand loyalty in some regions. Investors and shareholders also raised concerns about the company's sustainability practices, leading to questions about its long-term viability and ethical standing.

Path to Redemption:

In response to the environmental and reputational challenges, Nestlé took significant steps to address the pollution caused by its palm oil supply chain. The company committed to a no-deforestation policy and pledged to source 100% sustainable palm oil by 2023. Nestlé also joined the Roundtable on Sustainable Palm Oil (RSPO), a multi-stakeholder initiative focused on promoting sustainable palm oil production.

To ensure compliance with its sustainability commitments, Nestlé engaged with its suppliers and conducted rigorous supply chain audits. The company emphasized transparency in its palm oil sourcing practices and shared progress updates with stakeholders.

Lessons Learned:

The Nestlé case study serves as a real-life example of the cost of pollution and environmental degradation in the supply chain sector. It highlights the significant financial and reputational risks that companies face when their supply chains are associated with harmful practices, particularly in relation to deforestation and greenhouse gas emissions.

The case study also emphasizes the importance of proactive sustainability measures, supply chain transparency, and collaboration with suppliers to drive positive change. By committing to sustainability goals, engaging with stakeholders, and taking tangible actions to address pollution, companies like Nestlé can work towards mitigating environmental impacts and preserving their reputation in an increasingly eco-conscious world.

Chapter 11: Challenges and Future Trends

As the logistics industry strives to embrace green practices and sustainable solutions, it faces various challenges and uncertainties. This chapter explores the obstacles in adopting green logistics, the role of government and policy changes, and the emerging technologies and trends shaping the future of sustainability in logistics.

11.1 Overcoming Obstacles in Adopting Green Logistics

(i) Initial Investment Costs: One of the primary challenges is the upfront investment required to implement green logistics strategies, such as adopting renewable energy sources, purchasing eco-friendly vehicles, and redesigning packaging. Overcoming this obstacle requires long-term planning and a focus on the cost savings and environmental benefits that will be realized in the future.

(ii) Limited Infrastructure: The lack of infrastructure, such as charging stations for electric vehicles or recycling facilities for specific materials, can hinder the adoption of sustainable practices. To address this, stakeholders must collaborate to invest in the necessary infrastructure and promote its widespread availability.

(iii) Changing Consumer Behavior: While an increasing number of consumers value sustainability, there is still a need to raise awareness and influence more customers to support eco-friendly companies and products. Logistics companies must engage in consumer education and transparent communication to build trust and loyalty.

(iv) Resistance to Change: Resistance to change within organizations can be a significant obstacle in adopting green logistics practices. To overcome this, companies need to foster a culture of sustainability, provide training and support, and incentivize employees to embrace eco-friendly initiatives.

11.2 The Role of Government and Policy Changes

(i) Regulatory Incentives: Governments can play a pivotal role in encouraging green logistics by offering financial incentives, tax breaks, or grants for adopting sustainable technologies and practices. These incentives can offset initial investment costs and promote widespread adoption.

(ii) Environmental Regulations: Strengthening and enforcing environmental regulations can compel logistics companies to prioritize sustainability and reduce their environmental impact. Governments can set ambitious emission reduction targets and establish penalties for non-compliance.

(iii) Public-Private Partnerships: Collaborative efforts between governments, industry associations, and logistics companies can drive sustainable policies and initiatives. Public-private partnerships can foster innovation, share best practices, and promote knowledge exchange.

11.3 Emerging Technologies and Trends in Sustainability

(i) Autonomous Vehicles: The rise of autonomous vehicles, particularly electric and hydrogen-powered ones, holds promise for reducing emissions and optimizing transportation efficiency. Autonomous trucks and drones could revolutionize last-mile deliveries, further improving sustainability.

(ii) Artificial Intelligence (AI): AI-powered algorithms can enhance route optimization, demand forecasting, and energy management, leading to more efficient logistics operations and reduced environmental impact.

(iii) Circular Economy: Embracing circular economy principles involves designing products and supply chain processes to minimize waste and maximize resource use. This trend can drive significant sustainability gains in the logistics industry.

(iv) Renewable Energy Advancements: Advancements in renewable energy technologies, such as more efficient solar panels and energy storage solutions, can further incentivize the integration of clean energy sources in logistics operations.

(v) Data-driven Sustainability: Utilizing data analytics and advanced monitoring systems can provide real-time insights into environmental performance, allowing logistics companies to make data-driven decisions and continually improve their sustainability efforts.

(vi) Green Certification Programs: The adoption of green certification programs and eco-labeling initiatives can help consumers identify and support logistics companies with demonstrated environmental commitments.

The future of green logistics lies in the integration of innovative technologies, regulatory support, and a collective commitment to sustainability. By overcoming challenges and embracing emerging trends, the logistics industry can lead the way towards a greener and more sustainable future.

11.4. Conclusion

Green logistics is no longer a mere aspiration; it has become an imperative for the logistics industry to address environmental challenges and create a more sustainable future. This journey towards sustainability requires a comprehensive approach, including adopting renewable energy, green transportation, eco-friendly packaging, and collaborative supply chain practices. By embracing technology, data-driven decision-making, and regulatory support, logistics companies can achieve a balance between environmental responsibility and financial viability.

As the logistics industry navigates the complexities of green logistics, it must overcome challenges, seize opportunities, and stay committed to its role in safeguarding the planet. By working together, embracing innovation, and adhering to sustainability principles, the logistics industry can pave the way for a more sustainable and environmentally conscious future. The journey towards green logistics is a continuous one, but the benefits it offers for both the environment and businesses make it a journey worth taking.

Chapter 12: Human-Centered Sustainability in the Supply Chain

In the quest for sustainability within the supply chain sector, it is crucial to shift the focus from solely environmental considerations to embracing a human-centered approach. This chapter explores the human cost of supply chain practices, delving into the impact on employment, workers' welfare, and the communities in which supply chains operate. It underscores the importance of fostering a sustainable supply chain that not only benefits the planet but also promotes the well-being and dignity of all individuals involved.

12.1 The Human Face of the Supply Chain

The supply chain is not just a network of products and processes; it is a web of people with diverse roles and responsibilities. From factory workers and farmers to logistics personnel and retail employees, human hands and minds power every step of the supply chain. Understanding and addressing the human dimension of the supply chain is essential for creating a sustainable and equitable system.

One of the critical aspects of human-centered sustainability is ensuring fair labor practices and upholding workers' rights throughout the supply chain. This section highlights the challenges faced by workers, such as long working hours, low wages, and unsafe working conditions, and highlights the importance of fostering safe, dignified, and inclusive work environments.

12.2 Empowering Communities and Local Economies

Supply chains can have far-reaching effects on the communities they operate in. This section highlights the social impact of supply chain practices on local economies, livelihoods, and cultural heritage. It emphasizes the need for companies to engage with and empower communities, fostering positive socio-economic development that respects local values and traditions.

12.3 Ethical Sourcing and Responsible Supplier Relationships

Ethical sourcing is a critical component of human-centered sustainability. This section highlights the challenges of ensuring responsible supplier relationships, avoiding exploitative practices, and supporting suppliers' efforts to meet sustainability standards. By prioritizing ethical sourcing, companies can contribute to improved working conditions and fair treatment of workers across the supply chain.

12.4 Diversity and Inclusion in the Supply Chain Workforce

Promoting diversity and inclusion within the supply chain workforce is essential for a sustainable future. This section highlights the benefits of diverse perspectives and inclusive workplaces, aiming to eliminate discrimination and create opportunities for all individuals, regardless of gender, ethnicity, or background.

12.5 Health and Well-being of Supply Chain Workers

The health and well-being of supply chain workers directly impact their productivity and overall quality of life. This section highlights the importance of providing access to healthcare, mental well-being support, and a healthy work-life balance within the supply chain sector.

12.6 Upskilling and Training for Sustainable Employment

As supply chains evolve, new technologies and practices emerge, necessitating continuous learning and upskilling. This section highlights the significance of providing training and development opportunities for supply chain workers, empowering them to adapt to changing demands and advance in their careers.

12.7 Stakeholder Collaboration for Human-Centered Sustainability

Promoting human-centered sustainability requires collaboration among stakeholders, including companies, governments, non-governmental organizations, and consumers. This section highlights the power of partnerships in driving positive change and fostering collective responsibility towards human well-being within the supply chain.

12.8 Conclusion

Embracing a human-centered approach in the supply chain sector is not just a moral imperative; it is an essential component of sustainability in all its dimensions. By prioritizing fair labor practices, empowering communities, and ensuring the health and well-being of workers, companies can create a supply chain that benefits people and the planet alike. As we journey towards a more sustainable future, let us not forget the human face of the supply chain and the profound impact our actions have on the lives of those who make it all possible.

Chapter 13: Conclusion

13.1 Recap of Key Green Logistics Principles

Throughout this book, we explored the realm of green logistics and its transformative potential in the logistics industry. Key principles that emerged include:

Recognizing the Importance: Green logistics is essential for addressing environmental challenges, reducing carbon emissions, and preserving natural resources.

Integrating Sustainability: Sustainability must be integrated into all aspects of logistics operations, from transportation and warehousing to packaging and supply chain management.

Adopting Renewable Energy: Embracing renewable energy sources, such as solar and wind power, can significantly reduce the carbon footprint of logistics operations.

Promoting Collaboration: Collaborative efforts with supply chain partners, customers, and governments are vital for driving sustainable initiatives and achieving collective environmental goals.

Harnessing Technology: Utilizing technology, such as IoT, big data analytics, and blockchain, can optimize logistics processes, enhance visibility, and promote sustainability.

Compliance with Regulations: Adhering to environmental regulations and reporting carbon footprints fosters environmental responsibility and ensures transparency.

13.2 The Roadmap to a Greener Logistics Industry

The journey towards a greener logistics industry is a dynamic and ongoing process. To create a roadmap for achieving sustainability, logistics companies should consider the following steps:

Step 1: Assess and Set Goals: Begin by conducting a comprehensive assessment of current environmental impact and setting ambitious sustainability goals.

Step 2: Embrace Technology: Embrace innovative technologies like IoT, data analytics, and renewable energy to drive efficiency and reduce environmental impact.

Step 3: Collaborate and Educate: Collaborate with supply chain partners, governments, and customers to promote sustainability and educate stakeholders about green logistics practices.

Step 4: Adopt Eco-Friendly Practices: Implement eco-friendly practices such as renewable energy integration, waste reduction, and sustainable packaging to promote a circular economy.

Step 5: Report and Measure: Regularly report on environmental performance and measure carbon footprints to track progress and identify areas for improvement.

Step 6: Compliance and Advocacy: Comply with environmental regulations and advocate for policies that support green logistics and sustainability.

13.3 Inspiring a Sustainable Future in Logistics

The logistics industry plays a pivotal role in building a sustainable future for our planet. By embracing green logistics principles, logistics companies can inspire a sustainable future by:

Reducing Carbon Footprint: Adopting eco-friendly technologies and practices can significantly reduce carbon emissions and combat climate change.

Preserving Natural Resources: Sustainable practices, such as recycling, waste reduction, and responsible sourcing, help preserve natural resources for future generations.

Enhancing Reputation: Embracing sustainability enhances a company's reputation, attracting environmentally conscious customers, partners, and investors.

Contributing to Global Goals: Green logistics aligns with global sustainability goals, such as the United Nations Sustainable Development Goals, contributing to a better world for all.

As each logistics company commits to a greener future, the collective impact will be transformative, shaping a more sustainable and resilient industry. By continually striving for improvement, adopting innovative technologies, and fostering a culture of sustainability, the logistics industry can be a driving force in creating a more environmentally conscious and responsible world.

As the logistics industry moves forward, it must remember that green logistics is not just a trend but a fundamental shift towards a more sustainable and ethical approach. By taking the principles and lessons learned from this book, logistics companies can inspire positive change and be catalysts for a greener future in the logistics industry and beyond.

The pursuit of green logistics is not just a necessity; it is a commitment to preserving our planet for generations to come.

Printed in France by Amazon
Brétigny-sur-Orge, FR